The Number Poems

MATTHEW WELTON was born in Nottingham, where he now lectures in creative writing at the University. His writing practice includes collaborations with musicians, visual artists and other writers. His interest in poetry has to do with explorations of the sounds of words and the possibilities of repetition. The Number Poems is Welton's third Carcanet collection. It follows his 2003 debut *The Book of Matthew* (winner of the Jerwood Aldeburgh First Collection Prize) and the critically acclaimed *We needed coffee but...* (a 2009 Poetry Book Society Recommendation).

'You're unlikely to read anything like it ... poems are rarely so curious, precise and committed to their enquiry.'

JACK UNDERWOOD on *We needed coffee but..*

'It arrives with a unique and distinct sensibility; his poems create their own evocative and elusive worlds. There is a kind of relaxed quizzical sensuality running throughout, an easy, compelling confidence.'

THE GUARDIAN on *The Book of Matthew*

T0098280

Also by Matthew Welton from Carcanet Press

We needed coffee but we'd got ourselves convinced that the later we left it the better it would taste, and, as the country grew flatter and the roads became quiet and dusk began to colour the sky, you could guess from the way we returned the radio and unfolded the map or commented on the view that the tang of determination had overtaken our thoughts, and when, fidgety and untalkative but almost home, we drew up outside the all-night restaurant, it felt like we might just stay in the car, listening to the engine and the gentle sound of the wind. (2009)

The Book of Matthew (2003)

The Number Poems

M ATTHEW W ELTON

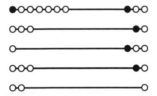

CARCANET

to Alison Henry, Kevin Chambers,
Paul Tornbohm and Pete Thompson-Swaine

First published in Great Britain in 2016 by
CARCANET PRESS LTD
Alliance House, 30 Cross Street
Manchester M2 7AQ
www.carcanet.co.uk

A CIP catalogue record for this book is
available from the British Library:
ISBN 9781784102203

The publisher acknowledges financial assistance
from Arts Council England.

Supported using public funding by
ARTS COUNCIL
ENGLAND

Contents

b

c

d

e

f

*

I

The book of numbers

Construction with phrases

Whatever I was thinking it was almost right:–
literature's for losers; religion makes us weak;
the mind's a kind of monkey with its teeth all gone.

I'm sitting in the kitchen with a pile of books
I thought I'd read but can't remember reading and
I'm wondering what's for supper 'cause I had no lunch

and when the monkey in the mind pulls up outside
and rubs his ribs and sucks his gums and says *Aw shucks,
we need to talk* – what else am I supposed to do

but give him coke and coffee till his words won't come?
The insects in the windows fill the air with thoughts.
The clouds are closing in on us. The sun looks lost.

TWO

I'm living in a lighthouse with a girl so tall
the heavens round her head surround her thoughts with stars.
I'm thinking of the sea-fish. I'm collecting rocks.

The summers last forever here, we like to think,
though when we go on picnics we expect some rain
and any day she's out of sorts her windfall words

come blurting out in blusters till her breath's all gone.
The days she takes the car to town my brains feel bruised
from wondering how she'll find her way, and what she'll spend,

and who she'll meet for lunch, and when I'm going through
her underwear the stacks of cards I find come signed
with love and logic, from the monkey in the mind.

THREE

The monkey in the mind expects [*no thoughts, no words,*
no sound, no speech the made-up rules [*no rain, no breeze,*
no dust, no sun] he sets out in his notebook as

his plane takes off [*no stars, no fish, no rocks, no light*]
should some day if he's lucky and the winds don't drop
[*no pull, no rub, no need*] be sure to bring about

[*no birds, no clouds, no wind, no towns, no trees, no hills*]
a kind of generous light [*no teeth, no love, no sense,*
no weight, no brains, no breath] like only God could give

[*no out, no in, no fit, no feel*] where what we want
we get [*no means, no moods, no books, no kids, no girls*]
and what we get [*no when, no what, no who*] we want.

FOUR

I'm trying out a treehouse for my girlfriend's kids
and all my dreams are treehouse-dreams where fraught blue birds
interrogate my motives for trashing her flat.

My girlfriend's kids spend summer-camp discussing how
the impact of the accident by which the words
enter our actual language might be minimised

by the innate aesthetic grasp which draws the mind
to imitate the functions of the parts of speech.
The monkey in the mind allows the day to cool

and fixes us a coffee and attempts to talk.
The breezes in the leaves create a sense of loss;
our moods show through like bruises, and the sun comes close.

FIVE

Whose words these are or how they work or what I want
to use them for, or why I've come to think it's more
the ritual than the spiritual that bears the weight

of how we square what we believe with how we live,
or how it is the static unemphatic fit
of word and sound and sound and thought and thought and word

says more about the language than the language could,
or if there isn't some way out of this, or if
the silence we return to makes the sound we make

feel freed by the conventions of the way we speak,
or what it is I think I'm saying here, means less
than less than nothing to the monkey in the mind.

SIX

And while we're at it, something in my fraughtest thoughts
questions the sense we make of what we make our words
and grows somewhat insistent that the talk we talk

is formed of nothing firmer than the blasts of dust
that rush at us like rumours through the low blue hills.
The clouds collect in clusters, and a slow breeze comes.

The monkey in the mind suggests that, most days now,
whenever I've been speaking I've become unclear.
I think that what I'm saying with the words I use

is stuff which, by the sound of things, I might not mean.
The insects fill the kitchen with their insect talk.
Is there more coffee? I think I need more coffee.

Hey, hey

Think of it as the rubber ball we've hidden
in the fruit bowl. Think of it as sludgy coffee.
Think of it like it's a bunch of balloons.

Imagine it's the voices on the recordings
we deleted. Think of it as the empty roads
you see from the empty train.

Think of it as the lull between your morning
at the typewriter and the hour you spend rehearsing
what you'll say you did with the cash.

Think of it as silty coffee. Imagine it as
telephone talk. It's the doodles in the condensation.
It's the bunches of plums overhanging the stream.

Think of it as the moment where our thoughts
thin out or the rain relents or the wagtails
huddle in the midsummer shadows, or, as the sparrows

go spiralling away from us, the raspberries redden
and the yellow weeds wilt, and we think of it
as a discontinuity in the discontinuity between things.

Think of it as a melody you'll muddle
on the cello – imagine it meandering like
thunder or thought. It's midsummer moonlight.

It's a ball of blue twine. Think of it
as gloopy coffee. Imagine it's imaginable. Think of it
as a lemon, and give it another squeeze.

Abstraction with instructions

A thing at its time is a continuation of itself, and a thing after its time is a continuation of itself; a thing is a continuation of the things within it, and a thing is a continuation of the things around it.

The hum which seems to emanate from things and the hum from which things seem to emanate fall into a kind of harmony or, possibly, we guess, the harmony of a harmony.

The weight of thought gives way to the greater weight of thoughtlessness, and the weight of things gives way to the greater weight of nothing.

The idea of the thing and the thing the thing is develop in different parallels and, necessarily, never meet.

By the most precise measure to the soberest mind in the clearest light the indistinction between things is at its most complete.

One thing drifts into another, and another into another, and whatever we begin and end with becomes, very definitely, indefinable.

I must say that at first it was difficult work #2

A delay, a diversion, a detour, a search
A dictator who earns what his citizens earn
A Jamaican, a German, a Chilean, a Turk
Amadeus, Amadeus, Amadeus, Wolfgang
A masala whose effects include delirium of the nerves
From my spaceship the earth appears distant and blurred

Gaining weight after thirty becomes tricky, I've heard
He's a sailor who's served with the naval reserve
Himalayas, unfeasible; Irrawaddy, unwise
If today was a Thursday I'd be thinking the worst
If the stadium's cursed then the kickers are cursed
I'm afraid I've a taste for nutritional worms

I'm arranging your words into syllabic bursts
In a place where the surfers are quick to disperse
It's a nurse but it's not this particular nurse
It's a shame he's unnerved by the mythical curse
It's my failure to further this ridiculous research
Lemonade with a fizz that's decidedly weak

Marinating the turkey in bitterish herbs
My mistaken immersion in visceral nervousness
Potato or turnip, jicama or burdock
She's persuaded her friends I'm a miserable jerk
The delay in alerting the vicar can't hurt
The marimba player fluffs it in the diatonic verse

The mistaken impression that love's undeserved
The Mosaic laws favour a disciplined world
There's a hoard of some worth in our fiscal reserves
There's a state on the coast the militia usurped
There's no reason on earth to desist from the stir-fry
The sensation was worsened and indefinitely warped

Unassertive but earnest, febrile but assured
Undismayed, undeserving and deserving in bursts
Unrelated and turgid and wicked and terse
Was it Scooter and Fozzy or Piggy and Kermit
When she's praying her words become dissonant and slurred
You may say nothing further on kissing that girl

Twelve deflections

low cloud, cold toast
too much coffee
in the coffee

*

apricot tree
blossom the colour
of lichen

*

birdless back yard –
too early to be
this awake

*

nettles beneath
the raspberry canes
pebbles and slugs

*

the poplars
perpendicular
to their shadows

*

slow clouds, slow winds
paracetamol
and coffee

*

breakfast table
beer bottle
radiator heat

*

among the weeds
the onions
barely even green

*

a lemon on
the breadboard
a trickle of juice

*

tree-colour sparrow
in the
sparrow-colour tree

*

dusky morning
the weak coffee
and the headache

*

sudden cloud
and sudden sunlight
wasps at the milk

Construction with stencil

ONE

Exactly as I'm saying it, the sunset comes
and, with it, something analgesic mists my mind.
The freckled flies speckle the skies; the blackberries blush;

the blueberries bloom. A yellow swallow hollers in
a hollow yellow willow tree and, while I think
I'm thinking up some brash new algebraic breeze,

the gutsy grouchy slouchy kid checks through his notes
and calculates the angle and resistance and
velocity and swerves around the curves around

the middle of my mind. The light becomes lucid;
a gust of musty melody meshes the air.
The mind is multiplicity. I hope I'm home.

TWO

Exactly what I'm saying is: the sunset comes,
and, in it, something anaesthetic mutes my mind.
The flock of flies doubles in size; the blackberries bloom.

A budgie in the sludge begins a song so long
a heap of people hear it in the year it takes
and none of them remembers where they heard it first.

The seriously delirious kid lets out his breath
and stipulates the apples which he'll polish up
and juggle with the plums and crimson damsons at

the middle of my mind. The light grows alluvial;
a gust of hasty melody measures the air.
The mind is modulation. It's a short haul home.

THREE

Exactly, that I'm saying that the sunset comes
means something mostly anaphoric minds my mind.
The feisty flies philosophise on if and how

His fundamental faith in their intelligence
puts them above the other creatures God loves less.
A robin doubles over in a fast freak breeze.

The static idiomatic kid sits down to think
and dithers with ideas so dry they crumble up
like crayon-wax, and mostly go unnoticed at

the margins of my mind. The light grows allusive;
a gust of misty melody mellows the air.
The mind is mutability. I hopscotch home.

FOUR

Exactly as I'm saying how the sunset comes,
something exactly analytic meets my mind.
The colours of the evening sun surprise the flies

who stop and gulp like goldfish in their squares of air.
A sparrow in its narrow furrow sleeps so deep
I wouldn't want to wake it while I'm still unwell.

The zesty underdressed kid wants to ruck and run
and sets off at a wander round the yonder round
the pond around the middle of the middle of

the middle of my mind. The light becomes lurid;
a gust of rusty melody misses the air.
The mind is mutuality. I hitchhike home.

FIVE

Exactly as exactly it exactly for
Exactly comes exactly blue exactly black
Exactly some exactly thing exactly mind

Exactly thought exactly flies exactly skies
Exactly breeze exactly and exactly I
Exactly bloom exactly blush exactly mind

Exactly up exactly at exactly is
Exactly which exactly if exactly how
Exactly in exactly my exactly mind

Exactly gust exactly through exactly kid
Exactly with exactly the exactly light
Exactly of exactly home exactly mind

SIX

Exactly what I'm saying as the sunset comes
will come to mean, for me at least, a muddled mind.
The furthest flies materialise; the breezes ease;

the blueberries bruise. A yellow yaffle snaffles up
a pile of apple waffles and, I'd like to think,
takes comfort from my distant uninsistent thoughts.

The pensive unresponsive kid can't see how come
the interglobal glimmer which intensifies
the planet's rim could emanate from something from

the middle of my mind. The light becomes lousy;
a gust of fusty melody musses the air.
The mind is minimality. I'm halfway home.

Under Jack Wood

the mailbox disappeared. and the lemonade stand disappeared.
musicians who discuss their work disappeared.

a slice of apricot pie disappeared. sleep disappeared, and maps
                                                    disappeared.
the taxicab disappeared in 1954.

a girl who sleeps by the river disappeared.
the professor disappeared, riding a red tractor.

*

money disappeared. bad juju disappeared. crocodiles and cradles and
                                          language disappeared.
two socialists disappeared, and began drifting home.

artworks that hung on the wall disappeared. people who sit on low boxes
                                                    disappeared.
a stimulating game of ludo disappeared.

a good thing disappeared, and a disappointing thing.
sixteen or seventeen years disappeared.

*

the sketchbooks of architects disappeared gradually.
background disappeared, and burn-outs disappeared.

a novel disappeared, and a pack of cigarettes.
a pitcher of sugary coffee disappeared.

ambiguity disappeared, and model airplanes disappeared.
a bucket of insects disappeared overnight.

Instruction with obstructions

Sufficiently particularised, there are as many forms as there are things, and any similarity between two things is a similarity between forms.

The things that thought makes possible are made possible only by thought; the things that make thought possible are made possible only by practice.

For now we can do without the thing, and do without the idea of the thing, but the idea of the possibility of the thing is perhaps too much to give up.

In the imagination the imagination is a function of reality, but, in reality, the things we imagine can only come out of nothing.

Whatever our words refer to, or mean, or represent, the way we construct the distinctions between things relies wholly on our hunches.

The definable thing grows less definite than the smudges at its edges, and the smudges at its edges grow less definable almost indefinitely.

Poem in 72 words

Roosters roost
Swallows roost
Warblers roost
Ducks roost
Grouses roost
Crows roost

*

Roosters swallow
Swallows swallow
Warblers swallow
Ducks swallow
Grouses swallow
Crows swallow

*

Roosters warble
Swallows warble
Warblers warble
Ducks warble
Grouses warble
Crows warble

*

Roosters duck
Swallows duck
Warblers duck
Ducks duck
Grouses duck
Crows duck

*

Roosters grouse
Swallows grouse
Warblers grouse
Ducks grouse
Grouses grouse
Crows grouse

*

Roosters crow
Swallows crow
Warblers crow
Ducks crow
Grouses crow
Crows crow

Twelve restrictions

a grapefruit on
a table
the trickle of juice

*

warm rain
on the warm pavement –
ferret on a lead

*

spindly branches
tangled between
telegraph wires

*

in the rain
the teenager
running up to bowl

*

slow breeze
deep cloud
electric mower in the rain

*

flimsy poppies
in the flimsy wind –
low pale sun

*

empty tumbler
empty tumbler
empty tumbler

*

picnic bench breakfast
milky coffee
milky clouds

*

their shadows
perpendicular
to the poplars

*

cloudy morning
coffee
refrigerator hum

*

dozing on the steps
harmonica
in his hand

*

and the shadow
of the stack
of unreturned books

Construction with six constraints

Whatever it was that got into the wasps and muzzled their minds
and abandoned them in the bathroom, it feels lonely to watch them
drifting up to the mirror, and wavering a little, and drifting away.

*

The problem as the wasps see it isn't that we want them
out of the jam but that, for us, there's even any difference
between what's jam and what isn't. Clouds reposition themselves. The
                                             shadows dissolve.

*

The music inside a wasp's mind softens, leaving nothing but the sounds
of worms moving through the soil, puddles evaporating, a breeze
                                            becoming slower.
Apple sap dissolving. Grass drying out. The earth absorbing the fallen
                                            leaves.

*

In imagined sunlight an imagined wasp positioning itself in the actual
                                            grass.
In actual sunlight an actual wasp positioning itself in the imagined grass.
In actual sunlight an imagined wasp imagining itself disappearing into
                                            the air.

TWO

Something shifts out of place, and the sound that the wasps make
as they circle about beneath the kitchen light slows down so absolutely
that their humming becomes stuttering, and their stuttering
                                        becomes practically a sigh.

*

Birds on the driveway, papery yellow flowers, painted railings, a radio
                                        somewhere.
Clusters of raspberries; clusters of blue plums. The shadows of the wasps
on the patio slabs; the reflections of the wasps in the windows.

*

The version of the world in which the distances the wasps cover
aren't, as such, travelled by the wasps, but occur as the earth
repositions itself – nudging the neighbourhood closer. And the
                                        brambles. And the plums.

*

The leftover peaches in the drizzly sunlight, lemonade bottles, buckets
                                        of plums.
Fidgety blue birds. Weeds on the path. A newspaper on a bench.
And the wasps hanging like hunches. And the wind making no sound.

THREE

Like someone talking themselves to sleep and, as they wake, taking up
the same continuing sentence: the wasps forever unspooling the same
                                                     unendable thought,
circling above the patio table, circling above the dish of blue plums.

*

On a dusty August morning, the wasps clustering around the plum tree –
giving shape to the idea of diligence; on a dusty August morning,
the wasps outside the window – giving shape to the idea of disinterest.

*

A wasp in September considering whether it's the trickle of thick juice
on the skin of the plum catching the sunlight, or the sunlight
catching the trickle of juice. Birds sing all evening. A breeze resumes.

*

The version of the world from which we grasp that the wasps
approach each morning determined to improve on the previous day:
                                                   more lemonade;
more jam; fewer trips outdoors; maybe some time away from the
                                                   neighbourhood.

FOUR

The wasps at dusk, caught in the mix of what it means
to be forever at the window and forever under the plum tree, and
to weigh no more than whispers, and drift away in the wind.

*

The sound wasps make resembles talk, and the sound the wind makes
resembles the river. The clouds barely move all afternoon, and the outlines
of the houses across the park dissolve into the shallow blue dusk.

*

The distance between the tree and its shadow, and the distance between
the shadow and the low evening sun. Lawnfuls of apples, wispy nettles.
the movements inside a wasp's mind, and the movements of the wasp.

*

Beyond the window, the wasps. And beyond the wasps, the raspberry
                                                        patch.
Unwatered vegetables, clotheslines strung between garages, Aeroplane
                                noise, the unhurriable August heat.
Kids on a trampoline. Punctured bicycles. Acres of nothingness. Acres
                                                        of dust.

FIVE

The version of the world in which nothing exists but the horizontal.
The wasps in the dusk occupying the space where the weeds overrun
the curving gravel path – not exactly not moving, not exactly not still.

*

Sunlight sets in, and the whims the wasps pursue – centring in on
the blackberry patch, hovering around the yellowish plums – put
                                                them somewhere between
indecision and decision: casual in their intentions; casual in their actions.

*

Like some fidgety kind of idea that crops up out of nothing,
and circles like uncertainty, and never exactly gives up – the wasps in
                                                                September
in our rubbly stretch of garden, jutting into the bushes, appearing
                                                                indistinct.

*

We're sitting in the kitchen with the windows open while the wasps
we'd been expecting drift over to our neighbour's where – and this isn't
just a guess – the jam's unimaginable sickly, and there's probably
                                                nobody home.

SIX

The structures apparent in the things of the world are, we realise,
only instances of the realer, more abstract structure. The wasps,
                                        becoming distracted
by the lemonade bottles – beginning to understand something, beginning
                                        to give in.

*

Lemonade bottles. The blunt autumn sunlight. A stack of magazines.
                                        Unreadable letters.
Apples on the table. Voices from the other room. And a wasp
at the kitchen window, like something at the end of its elastic.

*

As if in nudging up to the windows – each morning from outdoors,
and from indoors each afternoon – the wasps weren't bothered about
                                        getting through
but, actually, are figuring out what reflections are. Daylight dissolves.
                                        Drizzle resumes.

*

And suddenly it's autumn, and suddenly it's dusk, and suddenly the wasps
shifting around in the kitchen doorway seem reluctant to move too much –
suspended between two kinds of nothingness, suspended between two
                                        kinds of nothing.

There to make the rest of us look bad

A church bell in summer. The sky like rumpled paper. A build-up of heat. Small pigeons. A bucket of plump clams.

On a mellow weekday afternoon Chester and McKinley are seen buying nasturtiums. Chester isn't untalkative. McKinley isn't unconcerned.

If they've got it in mind to walk home along the river, they may find their moods grow unexpectedly uneasy. On the plum trees the plums appear robust and unripe.

Chester has become precise about the kind of wine he'll drink. McKinley gets a buzz out of sprawling under a tree. The weekend arrives like a familiar dilemma. The windows swing open. It isn't far to the road.

Does coffee lift the spirits? McKinley sometimes wonders. Until August the city was unrecognisable. Chester can't finish his can of lemonade.

Blunt pencils and loud music become part of life. Chester and McKinley spend an evening in the kitchen. Bowls of white sugar. A grapefruit on the table. The light will fade abruptly. The candles blow out.

Obstruction with abstractions

A thing in context is a thing in itself, and a thing out of context is nothing.

A thing in context is a thing in itself, and a thing out of context is almost nothing.

A thing in context is almost a thing in itself, and a thing out of context is almost nothing.

A thing almost in context is almost a thing in itself, and a thing out of context is almost nothing.

A thing almost in context is almost a thing in itself, and a thing almost out of context is almost nothing.

A thing almost in context is almost a thing in itself, and a thing almost out of context is almost almost nothing.

DFW #2

Save me your toast and porridge
The days without swifts or swallows
Liquid, gaseous, solid

The crayfish, the mussels, the lobster
Dawdling into Bristol or Norwich
Pay me a postman's salary

It tastes like rust or garlic
Paper cocktail umbrellas
Sailing due East from the colonies

The phrasebooks were mostly colloquial
Dilapidated Leicestershire cottage
Pay me a doctor's salary

Pacing around Austin or Dallas
Dog daisies, dog whistles, dog collars
Unduly unsubtle or immodest

We're just mates with the hipsters from college
Three-day sponsored silence
Sailing due West from the colonies

Stadium rock for toddlers
Undated fossilised mollusc
Pay me the hustler's salary

The waitress felt lost outside Paris
The delay, the hesitation, the stoppage
A faded mustardy yellow

Twelve infractions

crabapple tree
lichen the colour
of blossom

*

sullen cloud
and sullen sunlight
wasps in the sink

*

kitchen counter –
the jam jar
entirely empty

*

our shadows
ride home on
the shadows of our bikes

*

alone on the lawn
with dandelions
in his hands

*

picnic bench breakfast
cloudy coffee
cloudy skies

*

sunlight through
the kitchen door
and we can't get warm

*

heaped on the path
enough leaves
to get lost in

*

tossing a plum
between one hand
and the other

*

flat roads, flat skies
sparrows at
the speed of our bikes

*

the smell of warm sewage
in the warm
summer winds

*

in the woods
after the rain
the rain still coming

Construction on six principles

ONE

The pan of pilchards steaming on the stove is real.
The milk jug's real. The phone call's real. My gut-ache's real.
The midges at the edges of my mind are real.

The rubber in my ribs is real; the drum kit on
the driveway's real; the city I'll arrive in's real.
The crickets singing crotchets in the rain are real.

The sulky monkeys scratching in the sand are real.
The coffee slops are real; the drowsy girls are real.
The mailman bringing bluebells to my door is real.

Appetite's real; conjecture's real; refusal's real.
The drowsy boys are real. Jerseys and jeans are real.
The thoughts that fade like fireflies from my mind are real.

TWO

A real bird flies the scarlet skies. Real parcels come.
A real amount of money gets me real blue cheese.
Real absent people occupy my absent thoughts.

The real desires I feel diffuse my real regrets
and occupy a space and shape somewhere my mind
has difficulty getting to, though, once it's there,

it's hard to think I'd ever find I'd need to leave.
Grapefruit are real. The grackles in the grass are real.
My real delay in writing meant things went unsaid.

A real voice on the phone requests a sum of cash.
Real peaches fill my paper sack. A real drawer slams.
The real imagined minnows swim my mainstream mind.

THREE

It's real to reach a juncture up to which we'd guess
the notion that our thoughts exist not in our minds
but stuck in some continuum out of which we grab

whichever fictive, factive figures meet our needs
is just some clumsy whimsy, but which, closer up,
looks like the loop which, once we're through it, makes the thrust

of how our thoughts take form resemble something rigged
to cut across the contours of the mind's few moods.
I sing real rhymes; I've flown real kites. The minims in

my mind are real and make me think my head's no place
for humming in. It's real to want to wait things out.
It's real to want to wander where the mind won't go.

FOUR

Real is the night. Real is the ground. Real is the hush
I think I hear whenever where I'm up to fits
the pattern of the patterns of the things I want

to think I want. Real was the rot that sank my yacht.
Real are the scowls of growling owls. Real is the talk
of mawkish hawks. Real are the queues to tell my news.

It's real to feel unready to admit how come
the thoughts I keep the closest are none of my own
but cluster up like clouds among the hawthorn hills

and drift in with the drizzle through my mudflat mind.
Milkshake is real. Muskrats are real. Mustard paste's real.
Real people kept me guessing, and my train's just gone.

FIVE

Daylight's not real; rainfall's not real; chlorine's not real.
The shrugs of bugs aren't real; the gasps of wasps aren't real.
The words I wrote this morning and crossed out aren't real.

The preconditions out of which our thoughts occur
are, in and of themselves, not real, though, where I'm most
aware of them, I think I try and act as though

I thought if I denied them I'd deny my mind.
Disruption's real; dispersion's real; incision's real.
Real reticence accounts for all my unread books.

Sugar's not real; paper's not real; delay's not real.
Real is the rush I'll sometimes feel between each breath.
It's real that once I'm out of here I'm gone for good.

SIX

Some of the days I'm woken by the phone are real.
Some of the nights I'm stranded in the snow are real.
Some smart remarks are real; some butterflies are real.

Some sounds are real. Some sleep is real. Some moods are real.
The roads we map and measure in our minds are real.
Jumping in front of trains is real, some of the time.

The brothers singing breves between the leaves are real.
Real are the things we leave unnamed. Smudges are real.
It's real to know a bluebird by the way it hums.

Afters are real. Posters are real. Sandpits are real.
The real mistakes I maybe make seem like some kind
of measure for the music which diverts my mind.

Protraction

the gesture which adjusts each thing to the things around it creates a reality so plausible that it is only when we doubt its existence that we even acknowledge that it exists at all

II

Melodies for the Meanwhile

a

A measure for the meanwhile

We're idling along the sidewalk while the woman who's wandered ahead
of us is mumbling something unhummable and scrubbing the grubs

from her hands. Behind us a garage door swings open. A smell like burned
onions blends into the air. The mornings the haze

makes our uncertainty feel unfounded we amble around in the rubbery
poppies and keep each other talking until the muddly stuff's all been said,

and while we're partially particular on how the thing that makes a thing
a thing is a matter of modulation, we don't necessarily recognise

the distinction between things, and we act as if we're distracted by the
insects in the breeze. The shadows scuffle together and our moods

become less uncertain. When we empty out the butter tub we do it
without thinking, and when we speak it's as if we're unsure we'll be heard.

A modesty for the meanwhile

We traded the trout-hooks for a trickle of beer, and bundled into the
lumber truck, and trundled away in the wind. Our kitbags

fill with crabapple peel. Sunlight weakens the windows. The mornings
the haze makes our habits feel unshiftable we amble

around in the rubbery tulips and keep each other talking until the fussy
stuff's all been said, and while we're particularly

incisive on how the thing that makes a thing a thing is a matter of
location, we don't necessarily recognize the imbalance

between things, and we act as if we're distracted by the poppies in the
window. The shadows riff together and our moods become less

habitual. When we portion out the apple flan we do it without thinking,
and when we speak it's as if we're unsure we'll be heard.

A methodology for the meanwhile

While the woman upstairs is weeding her window box we sneak in
through the parcel room and leave her the leftover pencils.

We reconnect the socket box. The cassette tape unspools. The mornings
the haze makes our movements feel unmappable we amble around

in the rubbery buttercups and keep each other talking until the sorry
stuff's all been said, and while we're incisively perceptive

on how the thing that makes a thing a thing is a matter of process we
don't necessarily recognize the shifts between things

and we act as if we're distracted by the poppies in the yard. The shadows
huff together and our moods become less movable. When we

manage without the syrup spoons we do it without thinking, and when
we speak it's as if we're unsure we'll be heard.

A manifesto for the meanwhile

We never particularly dither over whether to bother with watermelons,
though as the fuzzy summer sunlight fills the rubbly village street, it

doesn't particularly feel as if we'd dither over much. We shuffle through
the bundle of alphabet cards. Trains trickle over the rickety road.

The mornings the haze makes our memories feel inflexible we amble
around in the rubbery daisies and keep each other talking until the weepy

stuff's all been said, and while we're perceptively emphatic on how the
thing that makes a thing a thing is a matter of remit, we don't necessarily

recognize the distance between things, and we act as if we're distracted by
the poppies in our hands. The shadows muffle together and our moods

become less memorable. When we buy up all the honey knives we do it
without thinking, and when we speak it's as if we're unsure we'll be heard.

A mutuality for the meanwhile

We bluff our way in through the basement apartment, and pocket the
potato knives, and count through the cash on the table. We stuff ourselves

with sesame seeds. The freezer fills with sludgy soup. The mornings the
haze makes our intentions feel intractable we amble around

in the rubbery thistles and keep each other talking until the kooky stuff's
all been said, and while we're emphatically specific on how

the thing that makes a thing a thing is a matter of partiality, we don't
necessarily recognize the delineation between things,

and we act as if we're distracted by the poppies in the path. The shadows
bluff together and our moods become less intent.

When we cut back on the peanut paper we do it without thinking, and
when we speak it's as if we're unsure we'll be heard.

A multiplication for the meanwhile

The pollen makes us sullen and the coffee makes us talk, and we slouch around on the kitchen steps until the sunlight's almost unnecessary.

The afternoon heat seems to deepen our voices. Paper blows out into the unoccupied yard. The morning the haze makes our guesswork

feel infallible we amble around in the rubbery nettles and keep each other talking until the dorky stuff's all been said, and while

we're specifically approximate on how the thing that makes a thing a thing is a matter of abruptness, we don't necessarily recognise

the compatibility between things, and we act as if we're distracted by the poppies in the wall. The shadows ruffle together and our moods

become less guessable. When we pack away the lemon tins we do it without thinking, and when we speak it's as if we're unsure we'll be heard.

b

A muddle for the meanwhile

We never entirely dither over whether to bother with watercolours, though
as the scuzzy summer sunlight fills the dusty village streets

it doesn't particularly feel as if we'd dither over much. Our rucksacks fill with
windfall plums. Wasps nudge into the windows. The morning the damp

makes our panic feel unappeasable we stumble around in the straggly
poppies and keep each other talking until the sneaky stuff's all been said, and

while we're particularly perceptive on how the thing that makes a thing a
thing is a matter of manipulation, we don't necessarily recognise

the continuities between things, and we act as if we're distracted by the tulips
in the window. The shadows clump together and our moods become less

panicky. When we manage without the butter spoons we do it without
thinking, and when we speak it's as if we're unsure we'll be heard.

A manoeuvre for the meanwhile

We're dawdling along the boardwalk while the woman who'd wandered
ahead of us is mumbling something unrepeatable and scrubbing the glue

from her hands. We reconnect the bicycle bells. Trailers trickle by on the
rickety road. The mornings the damp makes our analysis

feel unfollowable we stumble around in the straggly tulips and keep
each other talking until the giddy stuff's all been said, and while

we're incisively emphatic on how the thing that makes a thing a thing is
a matter of endurance we don't necessarily recognise

the implications between things, and we act as if were distracted by the
insects in the yard. The shadows clamp together and our moods

become less analytical. When we empty out the apple tub we do it without
thinking, and when we speak it's as if we're unsure we'll be heard.

A mortality for the meanwhile

We traded the tricycles for tropical fish, and bundled into the tulip truck, and trundled away in the wind. The afternoon heat seems to soften our voices.

A smell like burned plastic blends into the air. The mornings the damp makes our ideas feel unintuitive we stumble around

in the straggly buttercups and keep each other talking until the snarly stuff's all been said, and while we're perceptively

specific on how the thing that makes a thing a thing is a matter of wilfulness, we don't necessarily recognise the blur

between things, and we act as if we're distracted by the tulips in our hands. The shadows clog together and our moods become

less idealised. When we cut back on the syrup paper we do it without thinking, and when we speak it's as if we're unsure we'll be heard.

A monotheism for the meanwhile

We blag our way in through the riverfront apartment and pocket the
papaya knives and count through the cash on the table. Behind us

the oven door hangs open. Paper blows around in the unlit doorway. The
mornings the damp makes our tendencies feel improbable

we stumble around in the straggly daisies and keep each other talking
until the wary stuff's all been said, and while we're

emphatically approximate on how the thing that makes a thing a thing is
a matter of complexity, we don't necessarily recognise

the physics between things, and we act as if we're distracted by the tulips
in the path. The shadows clag together and our moods

become less tender. When we portion out the honey flan we do it without
thinking, and when we speak it's as if we're unsure we'll be heard.

A mitigation for the meanwhile

The apples make us unsupple and the coffee makes us itch, and we
slouch around on the kitchen steps until the sunlight's

almost unnoticeable. We shuffle through the boxes of telephone cards.
The satsuma peel uncoils. The mornings the damp makes our fixations

feel unfussy we stumble around in the straggly thistles and keep each
other talking until the untidy stuff's all been said, and while

we're specifically partial on how the thing that makes a thing a thing is a
matter of materiality, we don't necessarily recognise

the see-saw between things, and we act as if we're distracted by the tulips
in the wall. The shadows clip together and our moods

become less fixable. When we pack away the peanut tins we do it without
thinking, and when we speak it's as if we're unsure we'll be heard.

A metonymy for the meanwhile

While the woman upstairs is worming her whippets we sneak in through
the radio room, and leave her the leftover yarn. We cover ourselves

in cornflower seeds. The scrapbook fills with the photographs of
photographs. The mornings the damp makes our approaches feel

unfixable we stumble around in the straggly nettles and keep each other
talking until the sassy stuff's all been said, and while

we're approximately particular on how the thing that makes a thing a
thing is a matter of performance, we don't necessarily recognise

the traffic between things, and we act as if we're distracted by the tulips
in the breeze. The shadows cluster together and our moods

become less approachable. When we buy up all the lemon knives we do it
without thinking, and when we speak it's as if we're unsure we'll be heard.

c

A mumble for the meanwhile

We block our way in through the wintry apartment and pocket the pastrami knives and count through the cash on the table.

We reconnect the radiators. Trams trickle by on the rickety road. The mornings the traffic makes our intuition feel untenable

we rumble around in the scrawny poppies and keep each other talking until the messy stuff's all been said, and while we're incisively

specific on how the thing that makes a thing a thing is a matter of causality we don't necessarily recognise the concurrence

between things, and we act as if we're distracted by the buttercups in the yard. The shadows shunt together and our moods become

less intuitive. When we cut back on the butter paper we do it without thinking, and when we speak it's as if we're unsure we'll be heard.

A malevolence for the meanwhile

We never explicitly dither over whether to bother with water pistols, though
as the woozy summer sunlight fills the gravelly village streets it never

explicitly feels like we'd dither over much. The afternoon heat distorts our
voices. Paper blows out onto the uneven pathway. The mornings

the traffic makes our insistence feel ungrounded we rumble around in the
scrawny tulips and keep each other talking until the nervy stuff's

all been said, and while we're perceptively approximate on how the thing
that makes a thing a thing is a matter of malleability, we don't

necessarily recognise the congruities between things, and we act as if we're
distracted by the buttercups in our hands. The shadows shuffle together and

our moods become less insistent. When we manage without the apple
spoons we do it without thinking, and when we speak it's as if we're unsure
we'll be heard.

A makeweight for the meanwhile

We're sneaking along on the cakewalk while the woman who's wandering
ahead of us is mumbling something undoable and scrubbing the grit

from her hands. We worry ourselves over the watermelon seeds. The
dictionary wedges the window open. The mornings the traffic

makes our determination feel unmistaken we rumble around in the
scrawny buttercups and keep each other talking until the grizzly stuff's

all been said, and while we're emphatically partial on how the thing
that makes a thing a thing is a matter of determination, we don't necessarily

recognise the rifts between things, and we act as if we're distracted
by the insects in the path. The shadows shuttle together and our moods

become less determined. When we pack away the syrup tins we do it
without thinking, and when we speak it's as if we're unsure we'll be heard.

A marigold for the meanwhile

The truffles make us sniffle, and the coffee makes us drawl, and we slouch
around on the kitchen steps until the sunlight's almost

inconclusive. Our ladles fill with noodles. The benches fill with fidgety
kids. The mornings the traffic makes our doubts feel

interminable we rumble around in the scrawny daisies and keep each
other talking until the hassly stuff's all been said, and while

we're specifically particular on how the thing that makes a thing a thing is
a matter of attention, we don't necessarily recognise

the continuum between things, and we act as if we're distracted by the
buttercups in the wall. The shadows shorten together and

our moods become less dubious. When we empty out the honey tub we do it
without thinking, and when we speak it's as if we're unsure we'll be heard.

A materiality for the meanwhile

While the woman upstairs is wiping out the woodlice we sneak in through
the typewriter room, and leave her the leftover envelopes.

Behind us the locker door angles open. A smell like burned almonds
blends into the air. The mornings the traffic makes our confusion

feel unremarkable we rumble around in the scrawny thistles and keep
each other talking until the nutty stuff's all been said, and while

we're approximately incisive on how the thing that makes a thing a thing is
a matter of abstraction, we don't necessarily recognise

the space between things, and we act as if we're distracted by the buttercups
in the breeze. The shadows shamble together and our moods become less

confusable. When we buy up all the peanut knives we do it without
thinking, and when we speak it's as if we're unsure we'll be heard.

A manipulation for the meanwhile

We traded the trumpet for a spool of loose tripwire, and bundled into
the telephone truck, and trundled away in the wind. We shuffle

through the folders of algebra cards. The swimming towels unroll. The
mornings the traffic makes our interpretations feel imprecise

we rumble around in the scrawny nettles and keep each other talking
until the gawky stuff's all been said, and while we're partially

perceptive on how the thing that makes a thing a thing is a matter of
limitability, we don't necessarily recognise the forces between

things, and we act as if we're distracted by the buttercups in the window.
The shadows sharpen together and our moods become

less interpretable. When we portion out the lemon flan we do it without
thinking, and when we speak it's as if we're unsure we'll be heard.

d

A murmur for the meanwhile

The sorrel makes us feral and the coffee makes us mumble, and we
slouch around on the kitchen steps until the sunlight's almost irrelevant.

The afternoon heat seems to strengthen our voices. Paper blows about on
the unswept slabs. The mornings the temperatures make our instincts

feel unmanageable we scuffle around in the spiky poppies and keep each
other talking until the grotty stuff's all been said, and while

we're perceptively partial on how the thing that makes a thing a thing is
a matter of ordinariness, we don't necessarily recognise

the differentiation between things, and we act as if we're distracted by
the daisies in our hands. The shadows scrabble together and our moods

become less instinctive. When we pack away the butter tins we do it
without thinking, and when we speak it's as if we're unsure we'll be heard.

A mycology for the meanwhile

We blast our way in through the city-centre apartment and pocket the
paella knives and count through the cash on the table. We post

ourselves the poppy seeds. Daisies fill the marmalade jar. The mornings
the temperatures make our conclusions feel unpredictable

we scuffle around in the spiky tulips and keep each other talking until
the punchy stuff's all been said, and while we're emphatically

particular on how the thing that makes a thing a thing is a matter of
proportion, we don't necessarily recognise the ambiguities

between things, and we act as if we're distracted by the daisies in the
path. The shadows scram together and our moods become

less conclusive. When we cut back on the apple paper we do it without
thinking, and when we speak it's as if we're unsure we'll be heard.

A minimalism for the meanwhile

We never inherently dither over whether to bother with water-wings,
though as the drizzly summer sunlight fills the gritty village streets

it never inherently feels as if we'd dither over much. We shuffle through
the stack of measurement cards. The trikes trickle by on the rickety road.

The mornings the temperatures make our deductions feel unplottable, we
scuffle around in the spiky buttercups and keep each other talking until

the loony stuff's all been said, and while we're specifically incisive on how
the thing that makes a thing a thing is a matter of describability, we don't

necessarily recognise the slack between things, and we act as if we're
distracted by the daisies in the wall. The shadows scrape together and our

moods become less deductible. When we buy up the syrup knives we do it
without thinking, and when we speak it's as if we're unsure we'll be heard.

A meaninglessness for the meanwhile

While the woman upstairs is whistling along to the records we requested
we sneak in through the stationery room, and leave her the leftover

raspberries. We reconnect the water supply. The kettle flex uncurls.
The mornings the temperatures make our insights feel unstoppable,

we scuffle around in the spiky daisies and keep each other talking
until the feisty stuff's all been said, and while we're approximately

perceptive on how the thing that makes a thing a thing is a matter of
expansiveness, we don't necessarily recognise the unevenness

between things, and we act as if we're distracted by the insects
in the breeze. The shadows scrap together and our moods become less

insightful. When we manage without the honey spoons we do it without
thinking, and when we speak it's as if we're unsure we'll be heard.

A mannerism for the meanwhile

We traded the tractor for a small trombone and bundled into the laundry truck, and trundled away in the wind. Our forearms fill with grazes.

The windows withstand the fitful drizzle. The mornings the temperatures make our focus feel unemphatic we scuffle around

in the spiky thistles and keep each other talking until the unhappy stuff's all been said, and while we're partially

emphatic on how the thing that makes a thing a thing is a matter of provocation, we don't necessarily recognise the differentiation

between things, and we act as if we're distracted by the daisies in the window. The shadows scribble together and our moods

become less focusable. When we portion out the peanut flan we do it without thinking and when we speak it's as if we're unsure we'll be heard.

A marginality for the meanwhile

We're rattling along on the catwalk while the woman who wandered
ahead of us is mumbling something unspeakable and scrubbing the grass

from her hands. Behind us an aluminium door clangs open. A smell like
burned cinnamon blends into the air. The mornings the temperatures

make our assertions feel indescribable we scuffle around in the spiky
nettles and keep each other talking until the easy stuff's all been said,

and while we're particularly specific on how the thing that makes a thing
a thing is a matter of temper, we don't necessarily

recognise the traction between things, and we act as if we're distracted
by the daisies in the yard. The shadows scrum together and our moods

become less assertive. When we empty out the lemon tub we do it without
thinking, and when we speak it's as if we're unsure we'll be heard.

e

A melancholy for the meanwhile

While the woman upstairs is warming her wheatcakes we sneak in
through the cutlery room, and leave her the leftover elastic. We load

ourselves down with lawnseed. The branches fill with the silent finches.
The mornings the drizzle makes our assumptions feel unlikely

we muddle around in the droopy poppies and keep each other talking
until the quirky stuff's all been said, and while we're

emphatically incisive on how the thing that makes a thing a thing is a
matter of strategy, we don't necessarily recognise

the give between things, and we act as if we're distracted by the thistles
in the path. The shadows edge together and our moods become less

assumable. When we buy up all the butter knives we do it without
thinking, and when we speak it's as if we're unsure we'll be heard.

A modifier for the meanwhile

The pickles make us heckle, and the coffee makes us smirk, and we
slouch around on the kitchen steps until the sunlight's almost unsubtle.

We shuffle through the deck of requisition cards. The cotton sacks
come unbuttoned. The mornings the drizzle makes our conditions

feel unfeasible we muddle around in the droopy tulips and keep each
other talking until the gripey stuff's all been said, and while we're

specifically perceptive on how the thing that makes a thing a thing is a
matter of instruction, we don't necessarily recognise the contingencies

between things, and we act as if we're distracted by the thistles in the
wall. The shadows dredge together and our moods become less

unconditional. When we pack away the apple tins we do it without
thinking, and when we speak it's as if we're unsure we'll be heard.

A marsupial for the meanwhile

We blow our way in through the country apartment and pocket the
panini knives and count through the cash on the table. Behind us

the attic door flings open. Paper blows in from the unpainted kitchen.
The mornings the drizzle makes our disgruntlement feel unmistakable

we muddle around in the droopy buttercups and keep each other talking
until the gnarly stuff's all been said, and while we're approximately

emphatic on how the thing that makes a thing a thing is a matter of
procedure, we don't necessarily recognise the overlap between

things, and we act as if we're distracted by the thistles in the breeze.
The shadows smudge together and our moods become

less disgruntled. When we portion out the syrup flan we do it without
thinking, and when we speak it's as if we're unsure we'll be heard.

A makeover for the meanwhile

We traded the truffles for the coffee and waffles, and bundled into the
treacle truck, and trundled away in the wind. The afternoon heat

solidifies our voices. A smell like burned circuitry blends into the air.
The mornings the drizzle makes our methods feel uninventive

we muddle around in the droopy daisies and keep each other talking
until the nerdy stuff's all been said, and while we're partially

specific on how the thing that makes a thing a thing is a matter of
means, we don't necessarily recognise the nuances between

things, and we act as if we're distracted by the thistles in the window.
The shadows nudge together and our moods become

less methodical. When we cut back on the honey paper we do it without
thinking, and when we speak it's as if we're unsure we'll be heard.

A modernism for the meanwhile

We're chasing around on the crosswalk while the woman who wanders
ahead of us is mumbling something unthinkable and scrubbing the goo

from her hands. We reconnect the radios. Trolleys trickle by on the
rickety road. The mornings the drizzle makes our progress

feel immeasurable we muddle around in the droopy thistles and keep
each other talking until the skeevy stuff's all been said, and while

we're particularly approximate on how the thing that makes a thing a
thing is a matter of propulsion we don't necessarily

recognise the rub between things, and we act as if we're distracted by the
insects in the yard. The shadows sludge together and our moods

become less progressive. When we empty out the peanut tub we do it
without thinking, and when we speak it's as if we're unsure we'll be heard.

A moratorium for the meanwhile

We never exactly dither over whether to bother with watercress, though as
the fizzly summer sunlight fills the silty village streets it never

exactly feels as if we'd dither over much. Our jacket pockets fill with loose
chalk. The windows weaken the sunlight. The mornings the drizzle

makes our judgement feel unfathomable we muddle around in the droopy
nettles and keep each other talking until the dreary stuff's all been said, and

while we're incisively partial on how the thing that makes a thing a thing is
a matter of ratio, we don't necessarily recognise the affinities

between things, and we act as if we're distracted by the thistles in our
hands. The shadows fudge together and our moods become less

judgemental. When we manage without the lemon spoons we do it without
thinking, and when we speak it's as if we're unsure we'll be heard.

f

A meander for the meanwhile

We traded the treacle for tracing paper, and bundled into the pumpkin
truck, and trundled away in the wind. We shuffle

through the batch of dictionary cards. The kitchen window unlatches.
The mornings the mist makes our motions feel unfocused we fumble

around in the wispy poppies and keep each other talking until the funny
stuff's all been said, and while we're specifically

emphatic on how the thing that makes a thing a thing is a matter of
leverage, we don't necessarily recognise the interpolation

between things, and we act as if we're distracted by the nettles in the
wall. The shadows doodle together and our moods become

less motivated. When we portion out the butter flan we do it without
thinking, and when we speak it's as if we're unsure we'll be heard.

A minimum for the meanwhile

While the woman upstairs is wintering it out in the empty hotel up the
street we sneak in through the piano room, and leave her

the leftover muffins. Behind us the kitchen door springs open. A smell
like burned toffee blends into the air. The mornings the mist

makes our ambition feel unrealistic we fumble around in the wispy tulips
and keep each other talking until the zesty stuff's all been said, and

while we're approximately specific on how the thing that makes a thing a
thing is a matter of manner, we don't necessarily recognise the trickery

between things, and we act as if we're distracted by the nettles in the
breeze. The shadows puddle together and our moods become

less ambitious. When we buy up all the apple knives we do it without
thinking, and when we speak it's as if we're unsure we'll be heard.

A metricality for the meanwhile

The noodles make us dawdle and the coffee makes us dream, and we
slouch around on the kitchen steps until the sunlight's almost

ineffective. Our satchels fill with crayon sketches. The sidewalk fills with
the anxious girls. The mornings the mist makes our values feel

irreplaceable we fumble around in the wispy buttercups and keep each
other talking until the bossy stuff's all been said, and while we're

partially approximate on how the thing that makes a thing a thing is a
matter of statistics, we don't necessarily recognise the delineations

between things, and we act as if we're distracted by the nettles in the
window. The shadows muddle together and our moods

become less valuable. When we empty out the syrup tub we do it without
thinking, and when we speak it's as if we're unsure we'll be heard.

A mouthwash for the meanwhile

We're groping along on the ropewalk while the woman who'll wander
ahead of us is mumbling something indescribable and scrubbing

the grime from her hands. We save ourselves the sunflower seeds. The
smaller windows warp. The mornings the mist makes our consensus

feel impossible we fumble around in the wispy daisies and keep each
other talking until the risky stuff's all been said, and while we're

particularly partial on how the thing that makes a thing a thing is a
matter of gesture, we don't necessarily recognise the negotiation

between things, and we act as if we're distracted by the nettles in the
yard. The shadows noodle together and our moods

become consensual. When we pack away the honey tins we do it without
thinking, and when we speak it's as if we're unsure we'll be heard.

A momentum for the meanwhile

We never necessarily dither over whether to bother with the water rates,
though as the muzzly summer sunlight fills the pebbly village streets it

never necessarily feels as if we dither over much. The afternoon heat exhausts
our voices. Paper blows around on the unraked gravel. The mornings

the mist makes our responses feel inappropriate we fumble around in the
wispy thistles and keep each other talking until the huffy stuff's

all been said, and while we're incisively particular on how the thing that
makes a thing a thing is a matter of objective, we don't necessarily

recognise the premise between things, and we act as if we're distracted by
the nettles in our hands. The shadows swaddle together and our moods

become less responsive. When we manage without the peanut spoons we do
it without thinking, and when we speak it's as if we're unsure we'll be heard.

A mayonnaise for the meanwhile

We blunder our way in through the adjacent apartment and pocket the
paprika knives and count through the cash on the table. We reconnect

the record deck. The tractors trickle by on the rickety road. The
mornings the mist makes our decisions feel unintelligible

we fumble around in the wispy nettles and keep each other talking until
the weaselly stuff's all been said, and while we're perceptively

incisive on how the thing that makes a thing a thing is a matter of
activity, we don't necessarily recognise the tension between things,

and we act as if we're distracted by the insects in the path. The shadows
curdle together and our moods become

less decisive. When we cut back on the lemon paper we do it without
thinking, and when we speak it's as if we're unsure we'll be heard.

A note on the title

Maybe the idea was all about taxonomy. Maybe it was to do with finding a way of labelling these poems in a way that would emphasise that, in their shape and size, each poem displays some kind of regularity. And maybe that was about making the case that these poems might operate within the context of other writing that uses regular, measurable verses or paragraphs or rhymes. Maybe it was about making the case that these poems could operate within the context of other kinds of work that use fixed numbers of instruments or shades of paint, or fixed durations of performance, or whatever. Maybe too it had to do with the describability of each of the poems, and the idea was that if the particulars of each poem could be set out abstractly – which parts of the vocabulary are repeated; how the syntax is restricted; whether the sounds the sentences make follow a given formula – then there would be something recognisable that would hold them together. Maybe the idea of taxonomy was also about underlining the ways the poems differ from one other, and making a distinction between, for example, poems with different numbers of lines or poems in different metres. Maybe, though, the taxonomy was flawed. Maybe it was actually the idea of taxonomy that was flawed. Maybe in putting together poems whose construction depends on the number of sentences they use, poems whose construction depends on the number of metrical feet and poems whose construction depends on a basic word count, the mixture of methodologies was sure to result in confusion. And maybe the idea of *number* wasn't entirely appropriate anyway. Maybe *mathematics* would have been a looser but more comfortable fit. Maybe the more precise the target, the greater the scope for missing it completely.

A note on the note on the title

If, as it has been said, a poem is an arrangement of words containing possibilities, then there is something possibly curmudgeonly in giving a book a title which appears to be pleading that it should be read in a particular way. For sure, the process of constructing some of these texts was affected by the constraint that they should come to a particular length, but that doesn't exclude the possibility that the poems' form might be understood to play a part of less significance than the ideas they discuss or the places, situations, predicaments, or whatever, I was intending to describe.

A note on the note on the note on the title

The swallows watch our swingball match and gather in the branches, brooding on whether the bearing of forces on objects outweighs the bearing of objects on forces.

Notes on the poems

NUMBER: While the poems 'Construction with phrases', 'Construction with stencil' and 'Construction on six principles' make use of accentual-syllabic metres, the length of the lines in 'Construction with six constraints' is determined by the number of words. Word-counts are also used in 'Hey, hey', 'A note on the title' and 'A note on the note on the title, and 'Twelve deflections', 'Twelve restrictions' and 'Twelve infractions' use syllabic metres. The form used in 'Melodies for the meanwhile' and 'A note on the title' is a function of the number of sentences.

SETS: The words deployed in 'Under Jack Wood' are all taken from the Summer 2011 edition of *Bookforum* and, except for the names of the two singers, the words deployed in 'There to make the rest of us look bad' are all taken from *The Kitchen Diaries* by Nigel Slater. The titles of the sections of 'Melodies for the meanwhile' are constrained by a principle of alliteration, for some reason.

SYMMETRY: 'Construction with stencil' is among the poems which, to some degree, are put together using translational symmetry. In 'Melodies for the meanwhile' it is rotational symmetry that is used.

Acknowledgements

'Construction with phrases', 'Construction with stencil' and 'Construction on six principles' were published as the pamphlet *Waffles* (F.U.N.E.X., 2012).

A number of the poems in 'Twelve deflections', 'Twelve restrictions' and 'Twelve infractions' were published in the anthology *Off the Beaten Track: A Year in Haiku* (Boatwhistle, 2016).

Versions of some sections of 'Melodies for the meanwhile' were broadcast on The Verb on BBC Radio 3 in 2013.

Some of these poems have been previously published in *Poetry Review*, *PN Review*, *Prac Crit*, *New Walk*, *The Moth*, and *1110*.

'DFW #2' is a version of 'DFW' by Sam Riviere.